Dear Parent:

Buckle up! You are about to join your child on a very exciting journey. The destination? Independent reading!

Road to Reading will help you and your child get there. The program offers books at five levels, or Miles, that accompany children from their first attempts at reading to successfully reading on their own. Each Mile is paved with engaging stories and delightful artwork.

Getting Started
For children who know the alphabet and are eager to begin reading
• easy words • fun rhythms • big type • picture clues

Reading With Help
For children who recognize some words and sound out others with help
• short sentences • pattern stories • simple plotlines

Reading On Your Own
For children who are ready to read easy stories by themselves
• longer sentences • more complex plotlines • easy dialogue

First Chapter Books
For children who want to take the plunge into chapter books
• bite-size chapters • short paragraphs • full-color art

Chapter Books
For children who are comfortable reading independently
• longer chapters • occasional black-and-white illustrations

There's no need to hurry through the Miles. Road to Reading is designed without age or grade levels. Children can progress at their own speed, developing confidence and pride in their reading ability no matter what their age or grade.

So sit back and enjoy the ride—every Mile of the way!

For Uncle Sam and Uncle Jerry
S.A.

To Mysia, my cat
I.B.

Library of Congress Cataloging-in-Publication Data
Albee, Sarah.
Ahoy, Uncle Roy! / by Sarah Albee ; illustrated by Ilja Bereznickas.
    p.   cm.—(Road to reading. Mile 2)
Summary: Although it makes his parents a little uneasy, Walter's favorite person
is his Uncle Roy, a pirate.
ISBN 0-307-26216-2 (pbk.)—ISBN 0-307-46216-1 (GB)
[1. Pirates—Fiction. 2. Uncles—Fiction.] I. Bereznickas, Ilja, ill. II. Title.
III. Series.

PZ7.A3174 Ah 2001
[E]—dc21   00-064668

A GOLDEN BOOK • New York
Golden Books Publishing Company, Inc. New York, New York 10106

ISBN: 0-307-26216-2 (pbk)
ISBN: 0-307-46216-1 (GB)

10   9   8   7   6   5   4   3   2   1

AHOY, UNCLE ROY!

by Sarah Albee

illustrated by Ilja Bereznickas

My name is Walter.

This is my Uncle Roy.

Next to Mom and Dad,
he is my favorite person.

Uncle Roy loves his job.

He gets to travel a lot.

He meets really
interesting people.

And his office has
a great view.

Plus, he says the pay
is terrific.

But no matter
how busy he is,
Uncle Roy always
remembers to write to me.

15

Uncle Roy says his job
is not easy.

Sometimes he has to
let people go.

And he and his boss
don't always see
eye to eye.

19

Some days can have
their ups and downs.

But he hardly ever
calls in sick.

When he's not away
on business,
Uncle Roy loves
to spend time with me.

He has taught me
so many things—

like how to save

for a rainy day,

and how to do neat tricks.

He even taught me
how to cook.

My parents say
I can be whatever I want
when I grow up.

I want to be
just like my Uncle Roy.